299
Funny
Jokes for Kids

I.P. Grinning
&
I.P. Factly

DEDICATION

To Jacob & Riley.

What happened to the man who crossed a T-Rex with a chicken?

He got tyrannosaurus pecks!

Why did the one-handed man cross the road?

To get to the second hand shop!

What did the rats play at recess?

Hide and squeak!

Why don't crabs share their food?

Because they're shellfish!

Why do dogs always run in circles?

Because they don't know how many sides a rectangle has!

Why was the alien green?

It hadn't taken its space sickness pills!

What do you call a man floating in the sea?

Bob!

Why does the ocean not allow underwater playgrounds?

It's afraid of sea-saws!

Why do you rarely see a lionfish?

They can't hold the rods with their paws!

What happened to the man who crossed a cockerel, a poodle and a ghost?

He got a cocker poodle boo!

Why do jockeys ride horses?

Because they are too heavy to carry!

Why do witches have to be careful never to get angry on a broomstick?

In case they fly off the handle!

Why would an octopus vs. squid war be terrible?

Because they are so well-armed!

Why wouldn't they let the butterfly into the dance?

It was a moth ball!

What do you call a male cow taking an afternoon nap?

A bulldozer!

Why was the glow worm unhappy?

She realized she wasn't that bright!

Why was the leopard wearing a striped jumper?

So he wouldn't be spotted!

Why was the baby ant confused?

Because all his uncles were ants!

Why was the cemetery crowded?

Everyone was dying to get in!

Doctor, doctor, I keep thinking I'm a snowman!

Keep cool and I'll be with you in a moment!

Why should you never go to a theater on the moon?

It lacks atmosphere!

Why was Baron Frankenstein good around strangers?

He could make friends easily!

What happened to the man who crossed a leaky faucet with a dinosaur?

He got a drip-lodocus!

History teacher: Why does history repeat itself?

Pupil: Because no-one listens in history lessons!

What do you call polar cows?

Eski-moos!

What do you call a bee born in May?

A maybe!

What happened to the man who crossed a Lego set with a snake?

He got a boa constructor!

Why don't chickens like humans?

We beat eggs!

Why don't donkeys make good dancers?

Because they've got two left feet!

Why don't elephants ride motorbikes?

They can't fit their trunks in the helmets!

What did the policeman do when he caught the elephant that ran away with the circus?

Told her to take it back!

What did the seaweed shout when a fish began to eat it?

Kelp! Kelp!

Why don't jockeys ride horses when the sun goes down?

They are scared of night-mares!

Why does a dog get so hot at the beach?

It wears a coat and pants!

What did the shark say to its heartbroken friend?

Don't worry there's plenty more fish in the sea!

What happened to the man who crossed a cat with a lemon?

He ended up with a sourpuss!

What kind of dinosaur was always hurting itself?

Really-saurus!

Why do fish stay away from restaurants?

They are scared of getting battered!

Why do the Amish ride horse and buggies into town?

Because they are too heavy to carry!

Why do koalas never wear socks?

They prefer bear feet!

Why do elephants sit still on marshmallows?

They don't want to fall in the hot chocolate!

What happened to the man who crossed a cat with knee-length shoes?

He got puss in boots!

Why do librarians often talk about silent vegetables?

Because they are always saying "Quiet peas"!

Why do male deer always need braces?

They have buck teeth!

History teacher: Where was the Declaration of Independence signed?

Pupil: At the bottom!

Why do museums have old dinosaur bones?

They can't afford new ones!

Why do cows like to do on a night out?

Go to watch moo-sicals!

Why do cows think they should group together in fields?

It's just what they herd!

What kind of dinosaur was always crashing trucks?

Tyrannosaurus wrecks!

Why did the wood worm spend most of its time alone?

Because it was always boring!

What happened to the man who crossed a cat with the New York Times?

He got a mews-paper!

Why didn't the two worms go on Noah's Ark in an apple?

Because they all had to go on in pairs!

Teacher: Where might you find the English Channel?

Pupil: I don't know, is it near the MTV channel?

Why do aliens wear helmets?

So they don't scare themselves when they look in the mirror!

Why did the viper not viper nose?

Because the adder, adder tissue!

Why did the witch travel on a broom?

She had nowhere to plug in the vacuum cleaner!

Why did the otter cross the road?

To get to the otter side!

Why did the owl say, "Quack, quack, tweet, tweet"?

It didn't give a hoot!

Why do elephants avoid the beach?

They can't keep their trunks up!

Why did the teacher describe the boy's test results as underwater?

Because they were below 'C' level!

What happened when 100 hares escaped from prison?

Police had to comb the area!

What happened to the man who crossed a T-Rex with a poet?

He got a rhymer-soar!

Doctor, doctor, I've been kicked out of the baseball team - I keep dropping the ball!

Don't worry - what you have is not catching!

Why did the goldfish sell its old tank?

It couldn't work out how to drive it!

Why did the crazy space alien eat a couch and three chairs?

It had a suite tooth!

Teacher: Where are the Great Plains?

Pupil: In the airport!

Why did the vampire go to the doctor?

Because of the coffing!

Why did the dinosaur never forget to lock its front door?

Because tyrannosaurus checks!

Why did the crab cross the beach?

To get to the other tide!

Why did the elephant paint its toenails red?

To hide in the cherry tree!

Why did the elephant paint its toenails lots of different colors?

To hide in a bowl of M&M's!

Why did the elephant run away from the circus?

It was tired of working for peanuts!

Why did the elephant wear pink scarf and gloves?

The purple ones were in the wash!

Teacher: When was the last time your eyes were checked?

Boy: Never... they've always been brown!

What happened when a man tried to cross a tiger with a sheep?

He had to get a new sheep!

What happened when an elephant sat in front of a policeman at the movies?

He missed most of the film!

What do you call a mosquito in a metal suit?

A bite in shining armor!

What do you call an ant that dodges school?

A tru-ant!

Doctor, doctor, I've got some strawberries stuck in my ear!

Let's see, I think I've got some cream for that somewhere!

Doctor, doctor, I can't get to sleep!

Lay on the edge of the bed and you'll soon drop off!

What happened to the man who crossed a cow and a chicken?

He got roost beef dinner!

Why did St. Patrick drive all the snakes out of Ireland?

It was too far to walk!

Why did the scientist cross the road?

It wanted to learn more about the lives of chickens!

Why did the ape try to cook on his head?

He thought he was a griller!

Why did dinosaurs have wrinkled skin?

They spent too long in the bath!

Why don't mice swim in rivers?

They're scared of catfish!

Why did dinosaurs paint themselves black and white and jump in rivers?

To confuse the crocodiles!

Doctor, doctor, I keep seeing the future!

When did this start?

Tomorrow!

Why did the elephant cover itself in custard?

To hide in the trifle!

Why are rabbits so good at math?

They are the quickest multipliers!

What happened to the man who crossed a T-Rex with the floor of a ship?

He got tyrannosaurus decks!

Why are school cooks so evil?

They beat eggs and whip cream!

Why are spacemen so successful?

They are always going up in the world!

What happened to the man who crossed a cow and an earthquake?

He got a milkshake!

Why are spiders like tops?

They are always spinning!

Why are postal workers afraid of dogs called Frost?

Because Frost-bites!

Why are pirates so cool?

Because they just "Arrrrr!"

What do you call a crate full of ducks?

A box of quackers!

Why do elephants have trunks?

So they have somewhere to put their clothes when they go on vacation!

Why are fish the cleverest creatures in the sea?

They're always in schools!

Why are big trees and little dogs similar?

They both have lots of bark!

Which animals are not very brave?

Cow-ards!

Why are crabs never homeless?

There is always a seabed for them!

Why are crustaceans so irritable?

They are crabby!

What happened in court when a man was attacked by leg-eating zombies?

He was left without a leg to stand on!

Doctor, doctor, I think I'm a window!

Tell me where the pane is!

Who lost her elephants, and didn't know where to find them?

Big Bo Peep!

Who make dogs itch and humans laugh?

The Flea Stooges!

Why did dinosaurs avoid the sea?

They thought there was something fishy about it!

Who plays in nets in the monster soccer team?

The ghoulie!

Who steal pigs?

Hamburglars!

Who was the greatest dog detective?

Sherlock Bones!

Why are elephants usually gray?

So if you drop one in the fruit bowl you can spot it!

What do you call a crazy chicken?

A cuckoo cluck!

Why do elephants have flat feet?

From jumping out of their tree-houses!

Who cut sheep's wool?

Baa-bers!

What kind of dinosaurs never shut up?

Dino-bores!

Which fish lives in a monastery?

A monkfish!

Which fish swims best above the water?

A sailfish!

Which dinosaur ate the best food in the Southern USA?

Tyrannosaurus Tex-Mex!

Which pets live in volcanoes?

Hot dogs!

What do ducks watch on TV?

Duckumentaries!

What happened to the chicken whose feathers were all pointing the wrong way?

She was tickled to death!

Where should a 500 pound alien go?

On a diet!

What happened to the man who crossed a vampire and a duck?

He got Count Quackula!

Where should you weigh whales?

At the whale-weigh station!

What dinosaur had a pet dog with no eyes?

It-never-saurus rex!

Where was the Declaration of Independence signed?

At the bottom!

Where do toads leave their coats?

In the croakroom!

Why do dogs bury bones in the back yard?

Because they are not allowed to bury them in the kitchen!

Where do tough chickens come from?

Hard-boiled eggs!

Where do vampires eat their school lunches?

At the casket-eria!

Where do you find dinosaur words?

In a thesaurus!

Where do you find giant snails?

At the end of giant's fingers!

Where do injured rabbits go?

The hopital!

What happened to the elephant on a crash diet?

It wrecked six cars, two trucks and a school bus!

Where do library books like to sleep?

Under their covers!

Doctor, doctor, I'm terrified of cats!

Don't worry, I've got the purr-fect cure for you!

Where do monsters keep their hands?

In a box with the rest of the collection!

What is a bee's favorite Asian country?

Stingapore!

Where do bees save their money?

In a honey box!

Where do birds invest their money?

In the stork market!

Where do ducks save their money?

In a river bank!

What happened to the elephant that was chasing a boy on a bicycle?

Nothing, elephants don't ride bikes!

Where do vampires keep their savings?

In a blood bank!

Where do fish go to wash and clean up?

A river basin!

What do you call a girl who stretches across the tennis court?

Annette!

What do you call an elephant that's striped with big teeth?

A tiger!

Where did the boy think chickens came from?

Eggplants!

Where did the general keep his armies?

In his sleevies!

What happened to the leopard that stayed in the bath for a month?

It came out spotless!

Doctor, doctor, I feel like a dog!

Sit!

Where did the lost cows of America go?

Nobody's herd!

When is a vampire most likely to bite you?

On Chewsdays!

When is it difficult to get on the moon?

When it is full!

When is it ok to throw water in your dad's face?

When his beard is on fire!

When should you give your goldfish fresh water?

When they've finished what they've got!

When do cows call the first day of the year?

Moo Year's Day!

When do ducks wake up?

At the quack of dawn!

What happened to the famous duck detective?

He quacked the case!

When do elephants have three trunks and twelve legs?

When there are three of them!

When do ghosts get up?

In the moaning!

When do hens wake up?

Seven o'cluck in the morning!

What happened to the man who crossed a wooden boy with a fish?

He made Fin-occhio!

When do kangaroos celebrate their birthdays?

On a leap year!

What's big, gray and flies without wings?

An ele-copter!

What's big, gray and goes round and round and round and round and round and round?

An elephant on a carousel!

What's big, gray and goes up when the rain comes down?

An umbrella-phant!

Doctor, doctor, will this cream help the itching?

I never make rash promises!

What's even more dangerous than being with a fool?

Fooling with a bee!

What's got four tentacles, a huge head and wants you to shock it?

An alien with hiccups!

Doctor, doctor, I occasionally turn into an invisible monster!

I'm afraid I can't see you now!

What kind of dinosaurs were the best triple jumpers?

Tricera-hops!

What's grey with red spots?

An elephant with measles!

What's purple or green and can be seen from space?

The grape wall of China!

What's smaller than an ant's mouth?

An ant's lunch!

Doctor, doctor, I'm having trouble with my breathing!

Don't worry we'll soon put a stop to that!

What happened to the hens that ate dynamite?

They eggs-ploded!

What's even worse than raining cats and dogs?

Hailing taxis!

What's gray has four legs and a trunk?

A mouse going on holiday!

What's gray with big ears and a trunk and goes boing! boing!?

An elephant on a trampoline!

What happened to the man who crossed an acrobat with a dinosaur?

He got a flip-Iodocus!

What's green and hairy and goes up and down?

A gooseberry in an elevator!

What's green and hangs about in trees?

Giraffe bogeys!

Doctor, doctor, sorry I'm late, my leg hurts!

Oh dear - another lame excuse!

What's green with five legs and goes up and down, up and down?

An alien stuck in an elevator!

What's huge with red spots and eats cars?

The greater red-spotted car-eater!

What do you call a man that keeps flatfish on his head?

Ray!

What do you call an elephant that never has a bath?

A smelly-phant!

What's huge with ten arms, twelve legs and goes... Beep! Beep!?

A monster in a traffic jam!

Why does no-one ever hear pterodactyls using the bathroom?

Because they have a silent P!

What's orange and sounds like a parrot?

A carrot!

Doctor, doctor, please help me out!

Of course, which way did you come in?

What happened to the little dog that met a lion?

He was terrier-fied!

What's big, green and highly dangerous?

An elephant in a fruit bowl with a rocket launcher!

What's black and flies with witches?

A witch's bat!

What type of sheep can jump higher than the moon?

All of them – the moon doesn't jump!

What warning sound do Australian dogs on bicycles make?

Dingo-ling!

What was the best dressed dinosaur?

Suit and tie-ceratops!

What happened to the man who crossed an island of dinosaurs with some pigs?

Jurassic Pork!

What was Captain Kirk doing when he went into the ladies bathroom?

Boldly going where no man has been before!

What should you do with a blue elephant?

Cheer it up!

What happened to the man who crossed a tyrannosaurus with the beach?

He got a dino-shore!

What should you do with a gray elephant that suddenly turns red?

Stop embarrassing it!

What should you do with a green elephant?

Leave it in the tree until it ripens!

What should you do with a purple elephant?

Stop it choking!

What should you do with a red elephant?

Get it out of the sun!

What should you do with a see-through elephant?

Run away! It's an elephantom!

What was Mickey Mouse doing on Neptune?

Looking for Pluto!

What was the best of the kissing dinosaurs?

Lip-lodocus!

Doctor, doctor, people think I'm a cow!

Pull the udder one!

What was the cat doing with cheese on its tongue and its mouth wide open?

Waiting with baited breath!

What do you call skeletons that stay in bed all day?

Lazy bones!

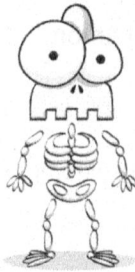

What was the dinosaur's favorite meal?

Jurassic pork!

What happened to the man who crossed a pig with Dracula?

He got a ham-pire!

What should you do with a white elephant with a yellow face?

Plant it in the garden and call it Daisy!

Doctor, doctor, I've just swallowed a pen – what should I do?

Use a pencil!

What side of a fish has the most scales?

The outside!

What do ghosts eat with meatballs?

Spook-etti!

What kind of wig can hear?

An earwig!

What kind of witch can you eat at the beach?

A sand-witch!

What kind pigs are always crashing their cars?

Road hogs!

What kinds of elephants live in the sea?

Wet ones!

What kinds of roads are known for their ghosts?

Dead ends!

What dinosaur only drinks small amounts of water at a time?

Sip-lodocus!

What kind of dog wears dark glasses and likes riding motorcycles?

A police dog!

What do you call an elephant in a fruit bowl with a rocket launcher!

Sir!

What lights spin around the Earth?

Satel-lites!

Doctor, doctor, my husband's feet smell of fish!

Poor sole!

History teacher: Where did the Pilgrims land when they got off the Mayflower?

Pupil: On the shore!

What lives in gum trees?

Mint flavored stick insects!

What kind of cat can perform somersaults and handstands?

An acro-cat!

What happened to the man who crossed a witch with a clock?

He got a brooms-tick!

What kind of cat has eight legs and squirts ink?

An octo-puss!

What kind of cat loves duck burgers?

A duck-filled patty puss!

What happened to the man who crossed a pit bull terrier and a seeing-eye dog?

It bit him then helped him to the hospital!

What kind of cat loves mail order magazines?

A cat-alog!

What kind of cats are disasters waiting to happen?

Cat-astrophes!

What kind of cats like to go ten pin bowling?

Alley cats!

Doctor, doctor, my boyfriends no good for me but I don't think I can dump him!

Take some of these and you'll soon feel like a new man!

What kind of cow eats the grass outside houses?

Lawn moo-ers!

What kind of dance do vampires enjoy?

The fang-dango!

What kind of dancing do young dogs like best?

Body-pupping

What is the difference between an invading alien fleet and a candy bar?

People like candy!

What is the difference between school dinners and elephant poop?

School dinners come on a plate!

What is the favorite color of a cat?

Purr-ple!

What is the first thing a dog does when it jumps in a lake?

Gets wet!

What is the first thing elves learn at school?

The elf-abet!

What is the male child of an ocean called?

Sea-son!

Doctor, doctor, I think I'm in church!

Just take a pew and I'll be with you in a minute!

What is the most important fish at a hospital?

A sturgeon!

What kind of dinosaur did secret work for the army?

Tricera-special-ops!

What is the name of the little rivers that flow into the Nile?

Juve-niles!

What is black, white, red and spotty?

A skunk with chicken pox!

What happened to the man who crossed a cat and a canary?

He got shredded tweet!

What is brown, rattles and says, "hith" "hith"?

A rattlesnake with a lisp!

What insect is bigger than an elephant?

A gi-ant!

What is even smarter than a talking bird?

A spelling bee!

What is fruity and kept in jars to stop them biting?

Jampires!

What is black, white and red all over?

A sunburnt penguin!

What is black and white, black and white, and black and white?

A penguin rolling down a hill!

What is a monster's favorite form of transport?

A chew chew train!

What do you call an exploding ape?

A baboom!

What is a young dog's favorite snack?

Pup-tarts!

What is a monster's favorite game at school?

Swallow the leader!

What is a nervous witch called?

A twitch!

What is a penguin's favorite hat?

An ice cap!

What dinosaur has a very firm handshake?

Grip-lodocus!

What do you do if a monster walks into your house and eats your brother?

Offer it your sister too.

What is an eagle's favorite TV show?

The feather forecast!

What is a polar bear's favorite meal?

Ice berg-ers!

What happened to the man who crossed a cat and a gorilla?

He got an animal that put him out at night!

Teacher: Why are you doing cartwheels in my class?

Pupil: I'm turning things over in my mind!

What happened when Baron Frankenstein saw a bare-necked corpse walking around?

He made a bolt for it!

What happens to vampires when they get tired?

They end up in a bat temper!

What do you call a man with a seagull on his head?

Cliff!

What do you call an ant with five pairs of eyes?

Antteneye!

Doctor, doctor, I think I'm an angel!

Well that's no reason to harp on about it!

What happens when a grape gets stood on?

It lets out a little wine!

What do you get when you fling a white stone into the Black Sea?

A wet stone!

What do you give an alien with six huge feet?

Three pairs of flippers!

What do you give an ill viper?

Asp-rin!

What do you have to take to become a proper witch?

Hexaminations!

What do you call a horse that lives next door?

A neigh-bor!

What do you call vampires in the mafia?

Fangsters!

Who was the cleverest monster maker ever?

Frank Einstein!

Where would you find an elephant?

Go back to where you left it then follow the trail of destruction!

What is brown and smells like red paint?

Brown paint!

History teacher: Who invented fractions?

Pupil: Henry the 1/8th!

What do you call young dogs playing in melting snow?

Slush puppies!

What do you call zombies that use phones?

Dead ringers!

What do you attract monkeys?

Sit on a branch and make a noise like a banana!

What do you do if a monster walks into your house and eats all your cakes?

Bake it some more!

Which hand should you always use to stroke a lion?

Someone else's!

What do you do when two snails fight?

Leave them to slug it out!

What happens when the dead get angry at Halloween?

They flip their lids!

What happens when you fling a white stone into the Red Sea?

It sinks!

What has 2 tails, 3 trunks and 7 feet?

An elephant with spare parts!

Why are ghosts so polite?

They don't spook until spooken to!

The End.

ABOUT THE AUTHOR

IP Grinning is the happy father of 7 and 9 year old boys. Their hilariously awful attempts to make up their own jokes inspired the IP Grinning & IP Factly series of joke books for kids.

Hopefully you'll enjoy this book as much as he enjoyed writing it.

CPSIA information can be obtained
at www.ICGtesting.com
Printed in the USA
LVOW13s0422170517
534792LV00008BA/361/P